CONTENTS

The Happy Life   1

Principal Teachings   10

Epicurus's Exhortations   23

Sayings of Epicurus in Greek Literature   40

Sayings of Epicurus in Cicero   46

Sayings of Epicurus in Seneca   51

The Fourfold Remedy by Philodemus   58

A Guide to Happiness

EPICURUS

A Phoenix Paperback

The abridged edition contains selected extracts
(with notes removed) from *The Epicurean Philosophers*,
edited by John Gaskin,
published by Everyman Paperbacks in 1995.

This abridged edition published in 1996 by Phoenix
a division of Orion Books Ltd
Orion House, 5 Upper St Martin's Lane, London WC2H 9EA

Translation of the Letter to Menoeceus and
translations from Cicero and Seneca © 1995 J. C. A. Gaskin

Cover illustration: 'Luncheon of the Boating Party,' 1880–81,
by Pierre Auguste Renoir (1841–1919), © Phillips Collection,
Washington D.C.
Bridgeman Art Library, London

ISBN 1 85799 597 X

Typeset by CentraCet Ltd, Cambridge
Printed in Great Britain by
Clays Ltd, St Ives plc

The Happy Life
(Letter to Menoeceus)

Introduction

Epicurus to Menoeceus, greeting.

No one should hold back from thinking about philosophy when young, nor in old age grow weary of the search for wisdom. It is never too soon or too late to secure the well-being of one's mind, and to say that the reason for studying philosophy has not yet come, or is already gone, is like saying that the reason for happiness is not yet come or is no more.

Therefore both old and young must study philosophy. The former so that, with advancing years, they may remain young in blessings through the joyous recollection of things past. The latter so that, while still young, they may at the same time be mature because they have no fear of things to come.

So we must meditate on what brings happiness, since if we have that, we have everything. And if we have it not, all our energies are directed at gaining it.

Whatever I have regularly commended to you,

practise and do, for what follows are the first principles of the good life.

The Gods are Blessed But of No Concern to Us

According to popular opinion, god is immortal and blessed. Accept this for a start. But do not then say of him anything that would be alien to his immortality and blessedness. Simply believe whatever is really consistent with it. For indeed gods exist. Our perception of them is clear. But they are not as ordinary people imagine, for they do not retain consistently their first impressions. Indeed he is not impious who destroys the gods of popular belief, but rather he who accepts the popular view. For the utterances of the multitude about gods are not true perceptions derived from sensation, but false assumptions: [For example] that the gods send the greatest rewards [to the good] and ultimate misery to the wicked (because the gods are always favourable to their own virtues and regard whatever is different as alien).

There is Nothing to Fear in Death

Get used to believing that death is nothing to us. For all good and evil lies in sensation and death is the end of all sensation. Therefore, a right understanding that death is nothing to us makes the mortality of life enjoyable, not by adding to it a limitless duration, but by taking away the yearning for immortality. For the man who has truly comprehended that there is nothing terrible in ceasing to live, has nothing terrible to fear in life. Thus a man speaks foolishly when he says he fears death. It will not pain him when it comes. It pains only in prospect. Whatever causes no distress when it is present, gives pain to no purpose when it is anticipated. Death therefore, the most dreaded of ills, is nothing to us. While we are, death is not; when death is come, we are not. Death is thus of no concern either to the living or to the dead. For it is not with the living, and the dead do not exist.

But generally, at one time a man will shun death as the greatest evil and at another long for it as a rest from the miseries of life. But the wise man neither looks for escape from life, nor for its cessation. Life does not offend him, nor does its absence look like any sort of evil. And just as men do not seek simply and only the largest portion of good but the pleasantest, so the wise seek to enjoy the time which is most pleasant and not merely that which is longest.

And he who advises the young to live well and the old to die well is foolish, not merely because life is desirable, but because the same training teaches us to live well and die well. Worse still is the man who says it were better never to have been born, and 'once born, make haste to pass the gates of Hades'. If he really believes this, why not act upon it? It is easy enough to do so if one is firmly convinced. But if he speaks insincerely, his words are folly among men who reject them.

Remember that the future is neither entirely ours nor entirely lost to us: we may not take its coming for certain, nor must we despair of it as quite certain not to come.

Blessedness is a Pain-free Body and a Tranquil Mind

We must consider some of our desires as natural and others as vain. Of those that are natural, some are necessary, others merely natural. Of necessary desires, some are necessary for happiness, others for the comfort of the body, others for life itself. A clear and positive understanding of these facts will enable each of us to direct every choice and avoidance in accordance with health for the body and tranquillity for the mind. For these are the objectives of a life of blessedness. For the end of all we do is to be free from pain and fear, and when once we have attained this, all turmoil of mind is dispersed and the living creature does not have to wonder as if in search of something missing, nor look for anything to complete the good of mind and body.

Pleasure is the Guide in All We Choose

When we suffer pain from the absence of pleasure, only then do we feel the need for pleasure. [But when we no longer feel the pain] we no longer need the pleasure. In this way, regard pleasure as the beginning and end of a blessed life. For we recognize pleasure as the primary and natural desire, and we return to it in all our judgements of the good, taking the feeling of pleasure as our guide.

But given that pleasure is the primary and natural good, we do not choose every and any pleasure, but often pass by many if they are outweighed by the discomforts they bring. And similarly we consider pain superior to pleasures when submission to the pains for a significant time brings a greater pleasure as a consequence. Thus every pleasure, because it is naturally akin to us, is good, but not every pleasure is fit to be chosen – just as all pain is an evil and yet not all is to be avoided. It is by comparison and by looking at the advantages and disadvantages, that all these things must be judged. For under certain circumstances we treat the good as an evil, and conversely evil as a good.

Live Simply

And again, we regard independence of external things as a great good, not so that in all cases we may enjoy only a few things, but in order to be contented with little if we have little, being honestly persuaded that they have the sweetest pleasure in luxury who least need it, and that all that is natural is easy to get, while that which is superfluous is hard. Once the pain due to want is removed, plain flavours give us as much pleasure as an extravagant diet, while bread and water bring the greatest possible pleasure to the life of one in need of them. To become accustomed, therefore, to simple and inexpensive food gives us all we need for health, alerts a man to the necessary tasks of life, and when at intervals we approach luxuries we are in a better condition to enjoy them. Moreover [simple things] fit us to be unafraid of fortune.

When we say that pleasure is the objective, we do not mean the pleasures of the profligate or the pleasures of sensuality, as we are understood to do by some through ignorance, prejudice, or wilful misinterpretation. By 'pleasure' we mean the absence of pain in the body and of turmoil in the mind. The pleasurable life is not continuous drinking, dancing and sex; nor the enjoyment of fish or other delicacies of an extravagant table. It is sober reasoning which searches out the motives for all choice and avoidance, and rejects those beliefs which lay open the mind to the greatest disturbance.

Live With an Eye to Consequences

Of all this, the beginning and chief good is care in avoiding undesired consequences. Such prudence is more precious than philosophy itself, for all the other virtues spring from it. It teaches that it is impossible to live pleasurably without also living prudently, honestly and justly; [nor is it possible to lead a life of prudence, honour and justice] and not live pleasantly. For the virtues are closely associated with the pleasant life, and the pleasant life cannot be separated from them.

The Happy Mortal

Who then is better than the man who holds right opinions concerning gods, who is entirely without fear of death, and who understands the highest good of nature? He understands how easily good things can be 7 attained and kept, and how pain is either short in duration or low in intensity. He laughs at [destiny] which some have set up as the ruler of all things. [He thinks that with us lies the chief power in determining events, some of which happen] according to natural law, others by chance, others through our own agency. He sees that natural law cannot be called to account for itself, that chance is inconstant, but that our own actions are free. It is to them that praise and blame naturally attach. It were better, indeed, to accept the myths about gods than to become a slave to the determinism of the physicists. At least the former holds out some faint hope if we placate the gods, while the latter is inescapable.

He does not regard chance as a god as most men do (for in the acts of a god disorder has no place) nor as an unstable cause. For he believes that good and evil are not dispensed to men by chance in order to make life blessed, although chance supplies the starting point of great good and great evil. He believes it is better to be unfortunate while acting reasonably than to prosper acting foolishly. It is better, in short, that what is well thought out in action [should fail, rather than what is ill thought out] should succeed by chance.

Meditate on these feelings, [Menoeceus], and on
8 things like them, by night and day, alone or with a

like-minded friend. You will then never be troubled in waking or in sleep, and will live like a god among men. For a man who lives among immortal blessings is unlike a mortal man.

Principal Teachings

I

A blessed and eternal being has no trouble himself and brings no trouble upon any other being; hence he is exempt from movements of anger and partiality, for every such movement implies weakness.

2

Death is nothing to us; for the body, when it has been resolved into its elements, has no feeling, and that which has no feeling is nothing to us.

3

The magnitude of pleasure reaches its limit in the removal of all pain. When pleasure is present, so long as it is uninterrupted, there is no pain either of body or of mind or of both together.

4

Continuous pain does not last long in the flesh; on the contrary, pain, if extreme, is present a very short time [because it kills], and even that degree of pain which barely outweighs pleasure in the flesh does not last for many days together. Illnesses of long duration even permit of an excess of pleasure over pain in the flesh.

5

It is impossible to live a pleasant life without living wisely and well and justly, and it is impossible to live wisely and well and justly without living pleasantly. Whenever any one of these is lacking, when, for instance, the man is not able to live wisely, though he lives well and justly, it is impossible for him to live a pleasant life.

6

In order to obtain security from other men any means whatsoever of procuring this is a natural good.

7

Some men have sought to become famous and renowned, thinking that thus they would make themselves secure against their fellow-men. If, then, the life of such persons really was secure, they attained natural good; if, however, it was insecure, they have not attained the end which by nature's own prompting they originally sought.

8

No pleasure is in itself evil, but the things which produce certain pleasures entail annoyances many times greater than the pleasures themselves.

9

If all pleasure had been capable of accumulation – if this had gone on not only by recurrence in time, but all over the frame or, at any rate, over the principal parts of man's nature, there would never have been any difference between one pleasure and another, as in fact there is.

10

If the objects which are productive of pleasures to profligate persons really freed them from fears of the mind, – the fears, I mean, inspired by celestial and atmospheric phenomena, the fear of death, the fear of pain; if, further, they taught them to limit their desires, we should never have any fault to find with such persons, for they would then be filled with pleasures to overflowing on all sides and would be exempt from all pain, whether of body or mind, that is, from all evil.

11

If we had never been molested by alarms at celestial and atmospheric phenomena, nor by the misgiving that death somehow affects us, nor by neglect of the proper limits of pains and desires, we should have had no need to study natural sciences.

12

It would be impossible to banish fear on matters of the highest importance, if a man did not know the nature of the whole universe, but lived in dread of what the legends tell us. Hence without the study of nature there was no enjoyment of unmixed pleasures.

There would be no advantage in providing security against our fellow-men, so long as we were alarmed by occurrences over our heads or beneath the earth or in general by whatever happens in the boundless universe.

When tolerable security against our fellow-men is attained, then (on a basis of power sufficient to afford support and of material prosperity) arises in most genuine form the security of a quiet private life withdrawn from the multitude.

Nature's wealth at once had its bounds and is easy to procure; but the wealth of vain fancies recedes to an infinite distance.

Fortune but seldom interferes with the wise man; his greatest and highest interests have been, are, and will be, directed by reason throughout the course of his life.

The just man enjoys the greatest peace of mind, while the unjust is full of the utmost disquietude.

Pleasure in the flesh admits no increase when once the pain of want has been removed; after that it only admits of variation. The limit of pleasure in the mind, however, is reached when we understand the pleasures themselves and their consequences – which cause the mind the greatest alarms.

Unlimited time and limited time afford an equal amount of pleasure, if we measure the limits of that pleasure by reason.

The flesh receives as unlimited the limits of pleasure; and to provide it requires unlimited time. But the mind, grasping in thought what the end and limit of the flesh is, and banishing the terrors of futurity, 15 procures a complete and perfect life, and has no longer any need of unlimited time. Nevertheless it does not shun pleasure, and even in the hour of death, when ushered out of existence by circumstances, the mind does not lack enjoyment of the best life.

21

He who understands the limits of life knows how easy it is to procure enough to remove the pain of want and make the whole life complete and perfect. Hence he has no longer any need of things which are not to be won save by labour and conflict.

22

We must take into account as the end all that really exists and all clear evidence of sense to which we refer our opinions; for otherwise everything will be full of uncertainty and confusion.

23

If you fight against all your sensations, you will have no standard to which to refer, and thus no means of judging even those judgements which you pronounce false.

If you reject absolutely any single sensation without stopping to discriminate with respect to that which awaits confirmation between matter of opinion and that which is already present, whether in sensation or in feeling or in any presentative perception of the mind, you will throw into confusion even the rest of your sensations by your groundless belief, and so you will be rejecting the standard of truth altogether. If in your ideas based upon opinion you hastily affirm as true all that awaits confirmation as well as that which does not, you will not escape error, as you will be maintaining complete ambiguity whenever it is a case of judging between right and wrong opinion.

If you do not on every separate occasion refer each of your actions to the end prescribed by nature, but instead of this in the act of choice or avoidance swerve aside to some other end, your acts will not be consistent with your theories.

All such desires as lead to no pain when they remain ungratified are unnecessary, and the longing is easily got rid of, when the thing desired is difficult to procure or when the desires seem likely to produce harm.

Of all the means which are procured by wisdom to ensure happiness throughout the whole of life, by far the most important is the acquisition of friends.

The same conviction which inspires confidence that nothing we have to fear is eternal or even of long duration, also enables us to see that even in our limited conditions of life nothing enhances our security so much as friendship.

Of our desires some are natural and necessary; others are natural, but not necessary; others, again, are

neither natural nor necessary, but are due to illusory

opinion. [Epicurus regards as natural and necessary desires which bring relief from pain, as e.g. drink when we are thirsty; while by natural and not necessary he means those which merely diversify the pleasure without removing the pain, as e.g. costly viands; by the neither natural nor necessary he means desires for crowns and the erection of statues in one's honour.]

30

Those natural desires which entail no pain when not gratified, though their objects are vehemently pursued, are also due to illusory opinion; and when they are not got rid of, it is not because of their own nature, but because of the man's illusory opinion.

31

Natural justice is a symbol or expression of expediency, to prevent one man from harming or being harmed by another.

32

Those animals which are incapable of making covenants with one another, to the end that they may neither inflict nor suffer harm, are without either justice or injustice. And those tribes which either could not or would not form mutual covenants to the same end are in like case.

33

There never was an absolute justice, but only an agreement made in reciprocal intercourse in whatever localities now and again from time to time, providing against the infliction or suffering of harm.

34

Injustice is not in itself an evil, but only in its consequence, viz. the terror which is excited by apprehension that those appointed to punish such offences will discover the injustice.

35

It is impossible for the man who secretly violates any article of the social compact to feel confident that he will remain undiscovered, even if he has already escaped ten thousand times; for right on to the end of his life he is never sure he will not be detected.

Taken generally, justice is the same for all, to wit, something found expedient in mutual intercourse; but in its application to particular cases of locality or conditions of whatever kind, it varies under different circumstances.

Among the things accounted just by conventional law, whatever in the needs of mutual intercourse is attested to be expedient, is thereby stamped as just, whether or not it be the same for all; and in case any law is made and does not prove suitable to the expediencies of mutual intercourse, then this is no longer just. And should the expediency which is expressed with the prior conception, nevertheless for the time being it was just, so long as we do not trouble ourselves about empty words, but look simply at the facts.

Where without any change in circumstances, the conventional laws, when judged by their consequences, were seen not to correspond with the notion of justice, such laws were not really just; but wherever the laws have ceased to be expedient in consequence of a change in circumstances, in that case the laws were for the time being just when they were expedient for the mutual intercourse of the citizens, and subsequently ceased to be just when they ceased to be expedient.

39

He who best knew how to meet fear of external foes made into one family all the creatures he could; and those he could not, he at any rate did not treat as aliens; and where he found even this impossible, he avoided all encounters, and, so far as was expedient, kept them at a distance.

40

Those who are best able to provide themselves with the means of security against their neighbours, being thus in possession of the surest guarantee, passed the most agreeable life in each other's society; and their enjoyment of the fullest intimacy was such that, if one of them died before his time, the survivors did not lament his death as if it called for commiseration.

Epicurus's Exhortations

All bodily suffering is negligible: for that which causes acute pain has short duration, and that which endures long in the flesh causes but mild pain.

*

It is hard for an evil-doer to escape detection, but to obtain security for escaping is impossible.

*

Necessity is an evil, but there is no necessity to live under the control of necessity.

*

[Remember that you are of mortal nature and have a limited time to live and have devoted yourself to discussions on nature for all time and eternity and have seen 'things that are now and are to come and have been'.][1]

*

For most men rest is stagnation and activity madness.

*

We are born once and cannot be born twice, but for all time must be no more. But you, who are not [master] of to-morrow, postpone your happiness: life is wasted in procrastination and each one of us dies without allowing himself leisure.

*

We value our character as something peculiar to ourselves, whether they are good and we are esteemed by men, or not; so ought we to value the characters of others, if they are well-disposed to us.

[1] Sayings in square brackets are by other Epicureans, and not by Epicurus himself.

*

No one when he sees evil deliberately chooses it, but is enticed by it as being good in comparison with a greater evil and so pursues it.

*

It is not the young man who should be thought happy, but an old man who has lived a good life. For the young man at the height of his powers is unstable and is carried this way and that by fortune, like a headlong stream. But the old man has come to anchor in old age as though in port, and the good things for which before he hardly hoped he has brought into safe harbourage in his grateful recollections.

*

Remove sight, association and contact, and the passion of love is at an end.

*

Forgetting the good that has been he has become old this very day.

*

We must not violate nature, but obey her; and we shall obey her if we fulfil the necessary desires and also the physical, if they bring no harm to us, but sternly reject the harmful.

*

All friendship is desirable in itself, though it starts from the need of help.

*

Dreams have no divine character nor any prophetic force, but they originate from the influx of images.

*

Poverty, when measured by the natural purpose of life, is great wealth, but unlimited wealth is great poverty.

*

You must understand that whether the discourse be long or short it tends to the same end.

*

In all other occupations the fruit comes painfully after completion, but in philosophy pleasure goes hand in hand with knowledge; for enjoyment does not follow comprehension, but comprehension and enjoyment are simultaneous.

*

We must not approve either those who are always ready for friendship, or those who hang back, but for friendship's sake we must even run risks.

*

In investigating nature I would prefer to speak openly and like an oracle to give answers serviceable to all mankind, even though no one should understand me, rather than to conform to popular opinions and so win the praise freely scattered by the mob.

*

[Some men throughout their lives gather together the means of life, for they do not see that the draught swallowed by all of us at birth is a draught of death.] 27

*

Against all else it is possible to provide security, but as against death all of us mortals alike dwell in an unfortified city.

*

The veneration of the wise man is a great blessing to those who venerate him.

*

The flesh cries out to be saved from hunger, thirst and cold. For if a man possess this safety and hopes to possess it, he might rival even Zeus in happiness.

*

It is not so much our friends' help that helps us as the confidence of their help.

*

We should not spoil what we have by desiring what we have not, but remember that what we have too was the gift of fortune.

*

[Epicurus' life when compared to other men's in respect of gentleness and self-sufficiency might be thought a mere legend.]

*

Nature is weak towards evil, not towards good: because it is saved by pleasures, but destroyed by pains.

*

He is a little man in all respects who has many good reasons for quitting life.

*

He is no friend who is continually asking for help, nor he who never associates help with friendship. For the former barters kindly feeling for a practical return and the latter destroys the hope of good in the future.

*

The man who says that all things come to pass by necessity cannot criticize one who denies that all things come to pass by necessity: for he admits that this too happens of necessity.

*

We must laugh and philosophize at the same time and do our household duties and employ our other faculties, and never cease proclaiming the sayings of the true philosophy.

*

The greatest blessing is created and enjoyed at the same moment.

*

The love of money, if unjustly gained, is impious, and, if justly, shameful; for it is unseemly to be merely parsimonious even with justice on one's side.

*

The wise man when he has accommodated himself to 30 straits knows better how to give than to receive: so great is the treasure of self-sufficiency which he has discovered.

*

The study of nature does not make men productive of boasting or bragging nor apt to display that culture which is the object of rivalry with the many, but high-spirited and self-sufficient, taking pride in the good things of their own minds and not of their circumstances.

*

Our bad habits, like evil men who have long done us great harm, let us utterly drive from us.

*

[I have anticipated thee, Fortune, and entrenched myself against all thy secret attacks. And we will not give ourselves up as captives to thee or to any other circumstance; but when it is time for us to go, spitting contempt on life and on those who here vainly cling to it, we will leave life crying aloud in a glorious triumph-song that we have lived well.]

*

We must try to make the end of the journey better than the beginning, as long as we are journeying; but when we come to the end, we must be happy and content.

*

You tell me that the stimulus of the flesh makes you too prone to the pleasures of love. Provided that you do not break the laws or good customs and do not distress any of your neighbours or do harm to your body or squander your pittance, you may indulge your inclination as you please. Yet it is impossible not to come up against one or other of these barriers: for the pleasures of love never profited a man and he is lucky if they do him no harm.

*

Friendship goes dancing round the world proclaiming to us all to awake to the praises of a happy life.

*

We must envy no one: for the good do not deserve envy and the bad, the more they prosper, the more they injure themselves.

*

We must not pretend to study philosophy, but study it in reality: for it is not the appearance of health that we need, but real health.

*

We must heal our misfortunes by the grateful recollection of what has been and by the recognition that it is impossible to make undone what has been done.

*

The wise man is not more pained when being tortured [himself, than when seeing] his friend [tortured]: [but if his friend does him wrong], his whole life will be confounded by distrust and completely upset.

*

We must release ourselves from the prison of affairs and politics.

*

It is not the stomach that is insatiable, as is generally said, but the false opinion that the stomach needs an unlimited amount to fill it.

*

Every man passes out of life as though he had just been born.

*

Most beautiful too is the sight of those near and dear to us, when our original kinship makes us of one mind; for such sight is a great incitement to this end.

*

Now if parents are justly angry with their children, it is certainly useless to fight against it and not to ask for pardon; but if their anger is unjust and irrational, it is quite ridiculous to add fuel to their irrational passion by nursing one's own indignation, and not to attempt to turn aside their wrath in other ways by gentleness.

*

Frugality too has a limit, and the man who disregards it is in like case with him who errs through excess.

*

Praise from others must come unasked: we must concern ourselves with the healing of our own lives.

*

It is vain to ask of the gods what a man is capable of supplying for himself.

*

Let us show our feeling for our lost friends not by lamentation but by meditation.

*

A free life cannot acquire many possessions, because this is not easy to do without servility to mobs or monarchs, yet it possesses all things in unfailing abundance; and if by chance it obtains many possessions, it is easy to distribute them so as to win the gratitude of neighbours.

*

Nothing is sufficient for him to whom what is sufficient seems little.

*

The ungrateful greed of the soul makes the creature everlastingly desire varieties of dainty food.

*

Let nothing be done in your life, which will cause you fear if it becomes known to your neighbour.

*

Every desire must be confronted with this question: what will happen to me, if the object of my desire is accomplished and what if it is not?

*

The occurrence of certain bodily pains assists us in guarding against others like them.

*

In a philosophical discussion he who is worsted gains more in proportion as he learns more.

*

Ungrateful towards the blessings of the past is the saying, 'Wait till the end of a long life'.

*

You are in your old age just such as I urge you to be, and you have seen the difference between studying 37 philosophy for oneself and proclaiming it to Greece at large: I rejoice with you.

*

The greatest fruit of self-sufficiency is freedom.

*

The noble soul occupies itself with wisdom and friendship: of these the one is a mortal good, the other immortal.

*

The man who is serene causes no disturbance to himself or to another.

*

The first measure of security is to watch over one's youth and to guard against what makes havoc of all by means of pestering desires.

The disturbance of the soul cannot be ended nor true joy created either by the possession of the greatest wealth or by honour and respect in the eyes of the mob or by anything else that is associated with causes of unlimited desire.

Sayings of Epicurus in Greek Literature

Freedom from trouble in the mind and from pain in the body are static pleasures, but joy and exultation are considered as active pleasures involving motion.

*

Sexual intercourse has never done a man good, and he is lucky if it has not harmed him.

*

I know not how I can conceive the good, if I withdraw the pleasures of taste, and withdraw the pleasures of love, and withdraw the pleasures of hearing, and withdraw the pleasurable emotions caused to sight by beautiful form.

*

The stable condition of well-being in the body and the sure hope of its continuance holds the fullest and surest joy for those who can rightly calculate it.

*

Beauty and virtue and the like are to be honoured, if they give pleasure; but if they do not give pleasure, we must bid them farewell.

*

The nature of the universe consists of bodies and void.

*

The nature of all existing things is bodies and space.

*

Think it not unnatural that when the flesh cries aloud, the mind cries too. The flesh cries out to be saved from hunger, thirst, and cold. It is hard for the mind to repress these cries, and dangerous for it to disregard nature's appeal to her because of her own wonted independence day by day.

*

It is better for you to be free of fear lying upon a pallet, than to have a golden couch and a rich table and be full of trouble.

*

Vain is the word of a philosopher which does not heal any suffering of man. For just as there is no profit in medicine if it does not expel the diseases of the body, so there is no profit in philosophy either, if it does not expel the suffering of the mind.

*

Let us at least sacrifice piously and rightly where it is customary, and let us do all things rightly according to the laws not troubling ourselves with common beliefs in what concerns the noblest and holiest of beings. Further let us be free of any charge in regard to their opinion. For thus can one live in conformity

with nature . . .

*

If God listened to the prayers of men, all men would quickly have perished: for they are for ever praying for evil against one another.

*

The beginning and the root of all good is the pleasure of the stomach; even wisdom and culture must be referred to this.

*

That which creates joy insuperable is the complete removal of a great evil. And this is the nature of good, if one can once grasp it rightly, and then hold by it, and not walk about babbling idly about the good.

*

It is better to endure these particular pains so that we may enjoy greater joys. It is well to abstain from these particular pleasures in order that we may not suffer more severe pains.

*

Let us not blame the flesh as the cause of great evils, nor blame circumstances for our distresses.

*

Nothing satisfies him for whom enough is too little.

*

Self-sufficiency is the greatest of all riches.

*

He who least needs to-morrow, will most gladly go to meet to-morrow.

*

The laws exist for the sake of the wise, not that they may not do wrong, but that they may not suffer it.

*

Even if they are able to escape punishment, it is impossible to win security for escaping: and so the fear of the future which always presses upon them does not suffer them to be happy or to be free from anxiety in the present.

*

A man who causes fear cannot be free from fear.

*

The happy and blessed state belongs not to abundance of riches or dignity of position or any office or power, but to freedom from pain and moderation in feelings and an attitude of mind which imposes the limits ordained by nature.

Sayings of Epicurus in Cicero

The wise man is little inconvenienced by fortune: things that matter are under the control of his own judgement and reason. No greater pleasure could be derived from an eternal life than is actually derived from an existence we can see to be finite.

*

The same way of thinking that reinforces our outlook so that we fear neither eternal nor long-term evil hereafter, has perceived that friendship is the strongest safeguard in this life.

*

If the things in which voluptuaries find pleasure could free them from fear of gods and death and pain, and if it could teach them to set bounds to their desires, we would have nothing to blame since on all sides they would be replete with pleasures, and on no side would they be vulnerable to pain or grief, which is the sole evil.

*

Epicurus to Hermarchus, greeting. I am writing in the course of the last and most blessed day of my life. I am suffering from diseases of the intestines and bladder which could not be more severe ... However, all these sufferings are compensated by the joy of remembering our principles and discoveries. But, as is appropriate in terms of the devotion you have displayed to me and to philosophy since your youth, please look after the children of Metrodorus ... My joy compensates the totality of pain.

*

Death touches us in no way; for what has suffered dissolution, is without sensation; and what is without sensation touches us in no way whatsoever.

*

[from Epicurus' last will] ... that his heirs Amynochus and Timocrates, in accordance with Hermarchus' 47 wishes, shall give enough for an annual celebration of his birthday in the month of Gamelion [namely January] and shall also assign a sum for a dinner for his fellow students in philosophy on the twentieth of each month, in order to keep alive the memory of himself and Metrodorus.

*

Nor yet for my part can I find anything that I can understand as good if I take away from it the pleasures afforded by taste, those that come from listening to music, those that come from the eyes by the sight of figures in motion, or other pleasures produced by any of the senses in the complete man. Nor indeed can it be said that joy of the mind all by itself is to be reckoned among [what is] good. For I recognize that a mind is in a state of rejoicing precisely when it has hope of all the pleasures I have spoken about. That is to say, the hope that nature will be free to enjoy them without any admixture of pain ... I have often asked those who are called wise what would remain in any good if they deducted from it the [pleasures] named (unless it were merely their wish to utter speech void of meaning). I have been able to learn nothing from these men. If they wish to continue prattling about virtues and wisdoms, they can mean nothing but the way in which the pleasures I have spoken about above can be effected.

*

Epicurus denies that a pleasurable life is possible unless lived with virtue. He denies that fortune has power over the wise. He prefers plain food to a rich excess. He denies that there can be any time when the wise man is not blessed.

*

That which is blessed and eternal may neither experience trouble itself nor extend trouble to others, and thus can feel neither anger nor favour, since anything like that is a weakness.

*

That which is finite has an end.

That which has an end can be perceived from [a point] external to itself.

But that which is everything [i.e., the universe] cannot be perceived from [a point] external to itself.

Therefore, since that which is everything has no end, [the universe] must necessarily be infinite.

Sayings of Epicurus in Seneca

Joyful poverty is an honourable thing.

*

Poverty conducted in accordance with the law of nature is great wealth.

*

This I wrote not for the money, but for you; for we are enough of an audience for each other.

*

You must be the slave of philosophy if you would enjoy true freedom.

*

Whoever does not regard what he has as the amplest wealth, though he be lord of the whole earth, yet is he wretched.

*

We ought to cherish some man of good character and have him always before our eyes, thus living as if he were watching us, and fashioning all our activities as if he could see them.

*

To live under constraint is an evil, but no one is constrained to *live* under constraint.

*

Among the rest of his faults the fool hath also this: that he is always *beginning* to live.

*

The fool's life is ungracious and fearful: it is directed
totally at the future.

*

If you live according to nature, you will never be poor; if you live according to opinions, you will never be rich.

*

For many, the acquisition of riches has not made an end of troubles, but an alteration.

*

Ungoverned anger begets madness.

*

Before you eat and drink anything, consider carefully who you eat and drink it with: for feeding without a friend is the life of a lion or a wolf.

*

Believe me, your discourse will seem more striking on a stretcher and in rags; for then it will not be a matter of lip-service but of actual experience.

*

[To Idomeneus, a once famous man] If you would be touched by fame, my letters will make you more renowned than all the things which you cherish and for the sake of which you are cherished.

*

If you wish to make Pythocles rich, be not adding to his money but subtracting from his desires.

*

No one departs from life in a state any different from that in which he entered it ... No one departs from life any different from how he was born.

*

It is irritating to be always starting to live ... They live badly who are always beginning to live.

*

It is ridiculous to run towards death because you are
tired of living, when by your manner of living you

have forced yourself to run towards death ... What is more ridiculous than to seek death when you have made your life unquiet by fearing it?

*

Do everything as if Epicurus were watching you.

*

Meditate upon death [Seneca offers the gloss 'It is a splendid thing to know well how to die'].

*

The time when you should most of all withdraw into yourself is when you are forced to be in a crowd.

*

Wealth is poverty adjusted to the law of nature.

*

Awareness of wrongdoings is the beginning of salvation.

*

I have never wished to please the crowd: for what I know, they do not approve; what they approve, I do not know.

*

First he hopes that there is no pain at the last breath; if however there is, he derives some comfort from its very brevity. For no pain which is severe lasts long. And in any event one will find relief at the moment of separation of body and life – even if it is terrible – in knowing that after this pain, no pain is possible. Nor does he doubt that life's breath in an old man is on his very lips, nor that but a little force is needed to disengage it from the body. 'A fire which has seized upon some flammable material needs water to quench it; but that which lacks sustaining fuel goes out of its own accord.'

*

Some people reach the truth without anybody's assistance and find their own way . . . some people need the help of others and won't go at all unless somebody goes ahead to them: but they are good at following.

*

[In Epicurus, there are two benefits which together constitute supreme blessings:] a body free from pain and a mind free from disturbance.

*

For the guilty to remain hidden is possible; to be confident in such concealment is impossible. [Seneca's gloss is 'Good fortune frees many men from punishment, but none from the fear of it.']

PHILODEMUS

The Fourfold Remedy[1]

Alpha
Nothing to fear in God.
Nothing to feel in Death.
Good can be attained.
Evil can be endured.

Beta
God is not worth fearing.
Death is not worth a worry.
But good can be attained,
And evil can be endured.

---

[1] Parts of the prose works of Philodemus (*c.* 110–30 BC) were recovered from charred papyrus rolls in Herculaneum. 'The Remedy', preserved in one of the Herculaneum rolls, is famous as a compressed account of Epicureanism. Alpha is Gilbert Murray's translation of a Greek original which differs slightly from the Herculaneum wording. Beta is an attempt to render the Herculaneum Greek.

Phoenix 60p Paperbacks

History/Biography/Travel
The Empire of Rome A.D. 98–190 *Edward Gibbon*
The Prince *Machiavelli*
The Alan Clark Diaries: Thatcher's Fall *Alan Clark*
Churchill: Embattled Hero *Andrew Roberts*
The French Revolution *E.J. Hobsbawm*
Voyage Around the Horn *Joshua Slocum*
The Great Fire of London *Samuel Pepys*
Utopia *Thomas More*
The Holocaust *Paul Johnson*
Tolstoy and History *Isaiah Berlin*

Science and Philosophy
A Guide to Happiness *Epicurus*
Natural Selection *Charles Darwin*
Science, Mind & Cosmos *John Brockman, ed.*
Zarathustra *Friedrich Nietzsche*
God's Utility Function *Richard Dawkins*
Human Origins *Richard Leakey*
Sophie's World: The Greek Philosophers *Jostein Gaarder*
The Rights of Woman *Mary Wollstonecraft*
The Communist Manifesto *Karl Marx & Friedrich Engels*
Birds of Heaven *Ben Okri*

Fiction
Riot at Misri Mandi *Vikram Seth*
The Time Machine *H. G. Wells*
Love in the Night *F. Scott Fitzgerald*

The Murders in the Rue Morgue *Edgar Allan Poe*
The Necklace *Guy de Maupassant*
You Touched Me *D. H. Lawrence*
The Mabinogion *Anon*
Mowgli's Brothers *Rudyard Kipling*
Shancarrig *Maeve Binchy*
A Voyage to Lilliput *Jonathan Swift*

POETRY

Songs of Innocence and Experience *William Blake*
The Eve of Saint Agnes *John Keats*
High Waving Heather *The Brontes*
Sailing to Byzantium *W. B. Yeats*
I Sing the Body Electric *Walt Whitman*
The Ancient Mariner *Samuel Taylor Coleridge*
Intimations of Immortality *William Wordsworth*
Palgrave's Golden Treasury of Love Poems *Francis Palgrave*
Goblin Market *Christina Rossetti*
Fern Hill *Dylan Thomas*

LITERATURE OF PASSION

Don Juan *Lord Byron*
From Bed to Bed *Catullus*
Satyricon *Petronius*
Love Poems *John Donne*
Portrait of a Marriage *Nigel Nicolson*
The Ballad of Reading Gaol *Oscar Wilde*
Love Sonnets *William Shakespeare*
Fanny Hill *John Cleland*
The Sexual Labyrinth (for women) *Alina Reyes*
Close Encounters (for men) *Alina Reyes*